Moving Water in Minecraft

Adam Hellebuyck and Michael Medvinsky

Published in the United States of America by Cherry Lake Publishing
Ann Arbor, Michigan
www.cherrylakepublishing.com

Reading Adviser: Marla Conn, MS, Ed, Literacy Specialist, Read-Ability, Inc.

Photo Credits: © Adam Hellebuyck and Michael Medvinsky/Cover, 1, 7, 18; © voyata/Shutterstock.com, 5; ©Mike Prosser/flickr, 8, 27; © Reece Bennett/flickr, 9; © Ecuadorpostales/shutterstock.com, 11; ©Gordon Wrigley/flickr, 13; © fiz_zero/Shutterstock.com, 15; © ANDREA DELBO/Shutterstock.com, 16; © Bernhard Klar/Shutterstock.com, 17; ©mrwynd/flickr, 19; © Phil's Mommy/Shutterstock.com, 21; © Agus_1899/Shutterstock.com, 23; ©MaggiCraft/flickr, 24; © MoreGallery/Shutterstock.com, 25; ©Bananinha God/flickr, 26; ©Noah Easterly/flickr, 29

Graphic Element Credits: © Ohn Mar/Shutterstock.com, back cover, multiple interior pages; © Dmitrieva Katerina/Shutterstock.com, back cover, multiple interior pages; © advent/Shutterstock.com, back cover, multiple interior pages; © Visual Generation/Shutterstock.com, multiple interior pages; © anfisa focusova/Shutterstock.com, front cover, multiple interior pages; © Babich Alexander/Shutterstock.com, back cover, front cover, multiple interior pages;

Library of Congress Cataloging-in-Publication Data
Names: Hellebuyck, Adam, author. | Medvinsky, Michael, author.
Title: Moving water in Minecraft: Engineering / by Adam Hellebuyck and Michael Medvinsky.
Description: Ann Arbor : Cherry Lake Publishing, [2019] | Series: Minecraft and STEAM | Audience: Grade 4 to 6. | Includes bibliographical references and index.
Identifiers: LCCN 2018035561| ISBN 9781534143142 (hardcover) | ISBN 9781534139701 (pbk.) | ISBN 9781534140905 (pdf) | ISBN 9781534142107 (hosted ebook)
Subjects: LCSH: Groundwater flow—Juvenile literature. | Irrigation—Design and construction—Juvenile literature. | Water and architecture—Design and construction—Juvenile literature. | Minecraft (Game)
Classification: LCC TC176 .H45 2019 | DDC 794.8/5—dc23
LC record available at https://lccn.loc.gov/2018035561

Printed in the United States of America
Corporate Graphics

Table of Contents

INTRODUCTION

People design things almost every day. If you have a new aquarium, you might have an idea of what you want it to look like. You might plan out how you want to arrange your fish's furniture—or even build a few pieces of your own! You'll have to work with the available space and the necessary equipment, like the water filter or heater. You might sketch all these ideas out.

The process of planning, building, and joining ideas and objects together is called engineering. People who do this for a living are called engineers. Engineers take ideas through phases. They have a dream, they **brainstorm** ideas, and they design the best idea they come up with. They then **prototype** and get feedback. Depending on the feedback, they either redesign the prototype or go back to the drawing board with a new dream or idea.

You may have found yourself going through a similar process when creating and building in *Minecraft*. Let's take a look at some ways you can use engineering ideas from real life to improve your building skills in the world of *Minecraft*.

There are many different and unique aquariums all around the world.

CHAPTER ONE

Irrigation: Ways to Move Water

Water is an important part of both the real world and in *Minecraft*. In the real world, water is needed for survival. It's needed for growing food and staying clean. Not all places in the world have easy access to water. Because of this, people have been figuring out how to move water from one place to another for thousands of years. When water is moved from one place to another to water crops, it is called **irrigation**. Irrigation systems were some of the first engineering projects and one of the world's biggest accomplishments.

> There are specific engineers who work together to think about how projects change the land around them. Environmental engineers work with designers to make sure their actions and creations do not have a negative impact on the environment. This **collaboration** may impact how a prototype is designed. Who can you work with to help make environmental decisions in *Minecraft*?

Having an irrigation system both in *Minecraft* and in the real world is important.

To keep predators away, you can build a moat around your home.

In *Minecraft*, water is used for many reasons. It is used to create new blocks, like obsidian, stone, and cobblestone. It can be used as an elevator to move things up or down. Water can even be used to trap mobs, animals, and monsters! And just like in real life, you can build an irrigation system in *Minecraft* to water your crops.

In the real world, there are two ways to move water from one place to another for people to drink. It is moved underground through pipes that carry the water to fountains and underground tanks. Or water is carried above ground in **aqueducts**. Big cities like New York City and Los Angeles use aqueducts to bring in water from the mountains and rivers in the countryside. Some aqueducts can be miles long. The longest aqueduct in the United States spans about 440 miles (700 kilometers).

A zombie that sinks in water will transform into a "drowned," a different type of zombie.

Before electricity, people relied solely on **gravity** to bring water to them. Engineers back then built large structures that sloped downhill so that the force of gravity could help water flow across long distances. In *Minecraft*, water also follows gravity. You may have seen water travel downhill several blocks when it is poured. You may also have seen waterfalls following gravity. How might you use this idea when building in the game? Can you use it to build your own aqueduct?

When designing irrigation systems and aqueducts, engineers don't just think about changing the location of the water. They also have to think about how their structures change the environment. For instance, in real life, animal and plant life may be negatively affected if too much water is moved from one place to another. Like us, they need water for survival.

You may have experienced this in *Minecraft* as well. Have you ever poured out a water bucket on a field filled with grass and flowers? You may have noticed that the water washes away all the grass and flowers. This is an example of how your actions in the game can impact the environment. The same thing can happen if you change the flow of water in *Minecraft*. Test this out. Try changing the direction of a river or a lava pool. Hint: Think like an engineer. Use the steps described in the introduction and in Chapter 2.

Early aqueducts, like the Cantalloc Aqueducts in Nazca, Peru, are still being used despite being built about 1,500 years ago!

ENGINEERING

There have been engineers who designed tools for moving water that **defy** the laws of gravity. They wanted to make water move up to higher places instead of down to lower ones. One of these designers was a man from Greece named Archimedes. Archimedes invented what is known today as the Archimedes screw. The device was made up of a long pipe and a screw. When the screw was turned, water moved up the pipe.

Archimedes invented his screw by building on the ideas of others. He got his idea by visiting Egypt. He saw how the Egyptians brought water from the Nile River to their gardens and fountains. He incorporated their system into his design.

Like Archimedes, engineers find solutions to problems. Many engineers combine other engineers' ideas and inventions to create something new or better. The process of building on other people's ideas has been used for hundreds of years and continues to drive **innovation** today. What problems do you see in your *Minecraft* world? How will you go about fixing them? Will you learn from other players? Will you experiment using your own designs?

While water is considered a block, it can only be collected using a bucket.

CHAPTER TWO

Architecture: Building in and Around Water

Engineers who design buildings are called **architects**. Architects often work on more than just buildings. They build roads, machines, bridges, tunnels, and other structures. They take many things into consideration when designing these structures, such as water. The design process often requires architects to work with or around water.

People have been using water for other purposes for thousands of years. Ancient Romans created hot relaxation rooms by running hot water through pipes under the floors and in the walls. Over time, engineers used similar ideas about water and heat to create inventions that keep people more comfortable during winter. For example, the boilers and radiators that heat today's homes use a process similar to what the Romans used to heat their rooms.

Some architects build structures that are best seen from above.

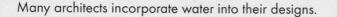

Many architects incorporate water into their designs.

You may have wanted to build a building or another structure in *Minecraft* but found that water got in your way. If you solved the problem by designing and building a structure that works with the water, you are thinking like an engineer!

Early engineers faced problems that were similar to what you may have encountered in *Minecraft*. These engineers wanted to float boats down long rivers, but there was an issue. The water levels were unequal in different parts of the river, which meant there were waterfalls, rapids, and sudden drops. This made it impossible for a boat to travel safely. Engineers solved this problem with the invention of locks. These locks acted like

Locks make traveling by water safer and easier.

There are many ways to build a water elevator in *Minecraft*.

miniature water elevators in the middle of the river. They raised and lowered boats in places where the water level suddenly changed. This invention is still in use today.

Have you ever tried to build a multilevel house in *Minecraft* but discovered you did not have enough room for a staircase? Have you ever wanted to build a unique way of traveling to your upper floors? You can approach these problems the way the engineers approached the river problem. You can build your own version of a water elevator in your *Minecraft* structure. By pouring a bucket of water into a tall, narrow space (maybe between floors of your house), you can float yourself up without needing stairs. This is one way to engineer a solution to this problem. What other ways could you engineer a solution?

Think about building a multilevel garden and irrigation system. What problems do you think you'll face?

CREATIVITY

Engineers have a specific way of thinking. They often use the design cycle when facing a problem. These steps are a way to break down a large problem into smaller pieces in order to solve the issue.

- Define a problem
- Research and gather information
- Brainstorm solutions
- Develop, plan, and build a prototype
- Test and share the prototype with others for feedback

You often act as an engineer and an architect in *Minecraft*. For instance, when you discover a problem you want to fix, you are defining a problem. This often leads you to do further research, like checking out *Minecraft* guides in the library. Gathering information and combining ideas moves you into the prototype phase, where you will make a first draft solution to the problem. This can be playing around with different blocks and tools to create a structure. Once you've created your first prototype, you will want to share it with others and get their feedback. Their ideas could spark new ideas of your own and have you thinking about your prototype in new ways. It could lead to an even better solution!

How do you solve a problem in *Minecraft*? What's your process?

CHAPTER THREE

Design: Incorporating Nature

Architects are always trying to improve buildings. They design new ones or redesign existing ones to make them interesting and unique. Some architects incorporate nature into their structures. For instance, if water is in or surrounding a potential building site, architects have important decisions to make. These decisions will affect what the structure will look like and how it will be designed. They can plan for the water to travel around the building, or they can creatively incorporate the water to flow throughout the building.

Frank Lloyd Wright was a famous architect who incorporated water in the many homes and buildings he designed. He designed over 1,000 structures in his life. Many of them were based on parts of the environment, like plants or water. His most famous building is called Fallingwater. Fallingwater is a house built in the Allegheny Mountains of

The sound of the waterfall can be heard from all areas in the house.

Pennsylvania on top of a waterfall. Wright built the house on and inside the waterfall, in a way that incorporated the natural environment.

The next time you build a home in *Minecraft*, think about how architects like Frank Lloyd Wright and engineers incorporate water and nature into their designs. Instead of building your house or structure next to the water, could you build it on top of the water?

Architects, engineers, and artists use elements like water to create optical illusions.

An infinity pool by a lake or ocean, both in *Minecraft* and in the real world, incorporate nature and the environment into its design by giving the illusion that it's part of a bigger body of water.

Designers often incorporate the environment into their work in creative ways. Have you ever been through a clear tunnel in an aquarium that lets you see the fish more closely? This is one example of creative design. Architects and engineers are always trying to improve their designs. They build glass floors in tall buildings or over water. They build pools that go from inside to outside or that merge into a lake or ocean. They have even built entire hotels underwater! How can you incorporate some of these engineering designs into your work in *Minecraft*?

What other parts of the environment could you build into your designs?

Extension Activity

You can use your engineering skills to solve problems in *Minecraft*. Think about the design process you learned about in this book.

Start by finding a problem you would like to solve in your *Minecraft* world. Is there a waterfall you would like to move? Do you want to build a city underwater?

Once you have chosen a problem, imagine some things you could do to solve it. Write these ideas down. Then look for information that can help you with your ideas. You could use the information in this book, in other books, or online to learn about different blocks or designs you could try.

After finding this information, build a sample of your idea in *Minecraft*. Once you have built it, ask other people to take a look at your design and suggest ideas for how to make it better. Your family and friends can be great resources. Based on what they say, you can change your sample design to make it better.

Keep doing this process until you have solved your problem. Try this with all kinds of different situations in the game. You will be amazed at what you can design and create!

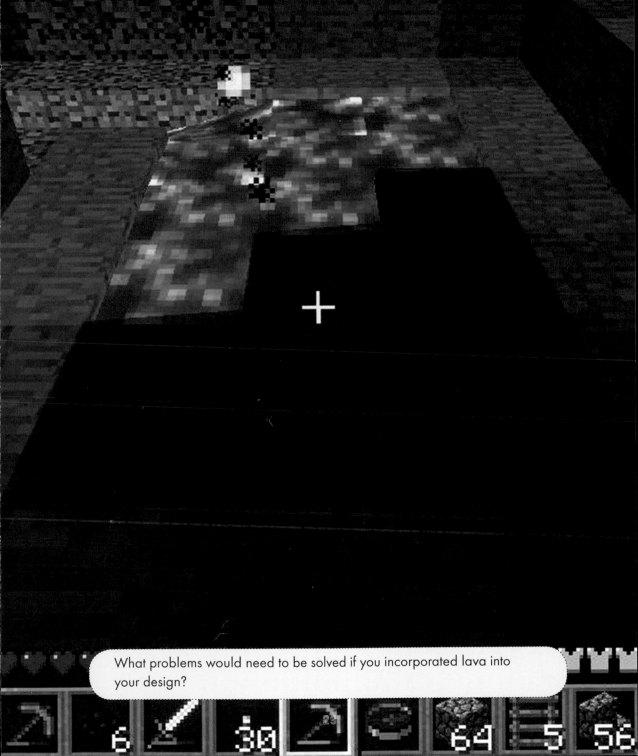

What problems would need to be solved if you incorporated lava into your design?

Find Out More

Books

Zeiger, James. *Minecraft: Mining and Farming*. Ann Arbor, MI: Cherry Lake Publishing, 2016.

Kelly, James Floyd. *Digital Engineering with Minecraft*. Indianapolis, IN: Que Publishing, 2016.

Websites

Minecraft Hour of Code Tutorials
https://code.org/Minecraft
This site will help you learn the basics of computer science and coding through *Minecraft*.

WonderHowTo—Techniques for Creating Architecture in Minecraft
https://minecraft.wonderhowto.com/news/techniques-for-creating-architecture-minecraft-0131731
Learn new ideas that can help you build in *Minecraft*.

Glossary

aqueduct (AK-wuh-duhkt) a man-made bridge with many arches moving water from one place to the other

architects (AHR-kih-tekts) people who design buildings

brainstorm (BRAYN-storm) to come up with ideas or solutions to a problem

collaboration (kuh-lab-uh-RAY-shuhn) working with others to make something

defy (dih-FYE) refuse to obey

gravity (GRAV-ih-tee) the force that attracts things to the center of the earth

innovation (in-uh-VAY-shuhn) a new idea, method, or device

irrigation (ir-uh-GAY-shuhn) moving water from one place to another

prototype (proh-tuh-TIPE) to create the first model of something

Index

Adam Hellebuyck is the dean of Curriculum and Assessment at University Liggett School in Grosse Pointe Woods, Michigan. Follow him on social media at @adamhellebuyck

Michael Medvinsky is the dean of Pedagogy and Innovation at University Liggett School in Grosse Pointe Woods, Michigan. Follow him on social media at @mwmedvinsky